AF291020

To my incredible parents.
N.L.

To Karolina – who always supports me
and makes me laugh.
G.H.

**With special thanks to Dr Jinx St. Léger
for her contribution and advice.**

First published 2026 by Nosy Crow Ltd
Wheat Wharf, 27a Shad Thames
London, SE1 2XZ, UK

Nosy Crow Eireann Ltd
c/o Fieldfisher Ireland LLP
45 Mespil Road,
Dublin 4, D04 W2F1, Ireland

www.nosycrow.com

ISBN 978 1 83994 116 0

Published by Nosy Crow in collaboration with the University of Cambridge.

A CIP catalogue record for this book is available from the British Library.

Printed in China following rigorous ethical sourcing standards.

1 3 5 7 9 8 6 4 2

UNIVERSITY OF CAMBRIDGE
nosy crow
PENICILLIN
AND OTHER
INCREDIBLE
MISTAKES
YOU'VE
(PROBABLY)
NEVER
HEARD
OF
Natalie Labarre
Gosia Herba

SSSSS
THE FACTORY OF FAILURE
SMILE
foot♡

Have you EVER made a mistake?

Like wearing your shirt inside out all day, pulling a 'push' door or even calling your teacher "Mum"? Well, you're not alone. Everyone makes mistakes sometimes . . . some are bad, some are lucky and some are INCREDIBLE!

Did you know that there are ALL SORTS of incredible mistakes you've probably never heard of?

AND SOME OF THEM HAVE SHAPED LIFE AS YOU KNOW IT!

One of the many mistakes that the explorer Christopher Columbus made happened when he saw manatees for the first time while sailing near the Dominican Republic. He mistook them for ugly mermaids, describing them as "not half as beautiful as they are painted".

In 2020, a French news site reported that about 100 famous people all died on the same day. Imagine the surprise for the 100 people who were in fact very much alive! The site had mistakenly released their prewritten obituaries!

**Can you spot these incredible mistakes?
Find them again later in the book
to learn more about them.**

- A broken toilet
- Crisps
- 'Lawn Chair' Larry
- Two dancing goats
- A painting in pieces
- The Leaning Tower of Pisa
- Dry cleaning
- A giant chicken

Mermaids aren't the only myth born out of a mistake. When people throughout history came across dinosaur fossils and reptile bones that they didn't recognise, stories of magical, scary dragons were born! You can't blame them - look at those things!

Since the 1980s, the swamps of southern Florida have been taken over by six-metre-long Burmese pythons! They were first brought over from Asia as fancy pets, but people soon realised how big they got and released them into the wild – a huge mistake!

Some blunders may be life-changing, but this one was LIFE-SAVING!

In 1928, biologist Alexander Fleming left a pile of dirty Petri dishes in his lab before going on holiday. When he got back, the dishes were covered in bacteria – no surprise – except for one. This special dish had a spot of mould on it, which had stopped the bacteria from spreading. What a way to discover the life-saving medicine **PENICILLIN**!

Would you believe, this was not the only discovery Alexander Fleming made by doing something a little icky. Once while he was working, a drip of his snot somehow made its way on to some bacteria. Gross, yes – but brilliant! After a few weeks, he realised that the bacteria were slowly dying away – mucus (snot) turns out to have a small amount of natural antiseptic called lysozyme which helps the body fight germs! Way to put the 'phlegm' in Fleming.

In 1895, Professor Wilhelm Röntgen was experimenting when something strange happened. As he passed electricity through a tube full of special gas covered in black card, somehow, a surface nearby started glowing. After more experiments, he used the invisible rays to take photos of the bones in his willing wife's hands! Since Röntgen didn't understand what he'd discovered yet, he called them **X-RAYS**!

While building a heartbeat-recorder in 1956, Wilson Greatbatch used the wrong part by mistake. His error gave the machine the rhythm of a human heart instead . . . bom bom . . . bom bom . . . These were the first beats of the **PACEMAKER**, a device that could be placed inside a person to keep their heart beating.

French chemist Édouard Bénédictus saved countless lives by being clumsy. In 1903, he accidentally knocked over a glass flask. But when he kneeled down to pick up the pieces, there weren't any. The flask was shattered but it had kept its shape thanks to a thin layer of plastic that had dried on the inside. His idea for **SAFETY GLASS** is now used to make car windows and shower doors safer.

Some mistakes work out for THE BEST

In 1856, chemist William Perkin was trying to create quinine, a chemical used in medicine. Instead, he made a dark, slimy, gooey mess that left purple stains on everything, but ended up taking the fashion world by storm! Perkin had accidentally invented a **DYE** that was more vibrant than the dyes of the time made from plants and bugs (ew).

In 1964, Donald Rusk Currey **ACCIDENTALLY CUT DOWN ONE OF THE OLDEST LIVING TREES** – a 4,900-year-old bristlecone pine named Prometheus. After counting its rings, he quickly realised what he'd done. Oh no! But what began as an outrage became an opportunity. Because of Donald's mishap, our planet's oldest trees are now protected, and their locations are kept secret so no one can hurt them.

Bobby Leach was a daredevil circus stuntman who spent his life doing one dangerous thing after another, like, oh, plummeting down Niagara Falls in a barrel, for example. No one would ever have guessed that he would finally die from something rather ordinary. Yep – in 1926, he slipped on an orange peel and that was that.

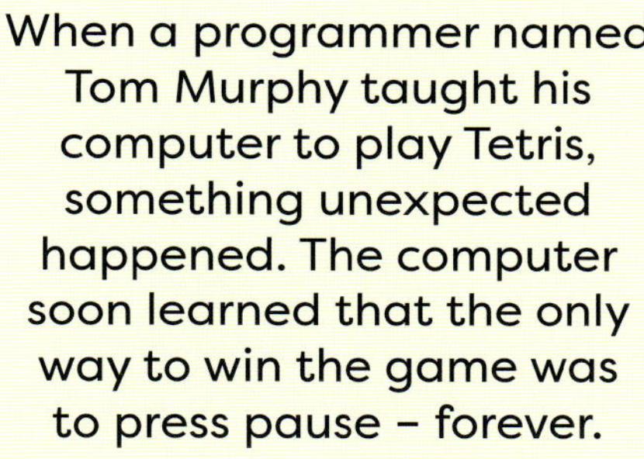

When a programmer named Tom Murphy taught his computer to play Tetris, something unexpected happened. The computer soon learned that the only way to win the game was to press pause – forever.

On a cold January afternoon in 1919, Boston was taken by surprise when a tidal wave of sweet, sticky molasses burst out of a storage container and **FLOODED THE STREETS.** The 12-metre-high, 50-metre-wide wave scooped up everything in its path. Decades later, locals swore they could still smell it on a hot day.

Take a peek inside your kitchen –
IT'S FULL OF MISTAKES!

In 1853, chef George Crum was angry. A fussy customer kept sending back his fried potatoes because they were too thick. To teach them a lesson, Crum sliced the potatoes so ridiculously thin that they were crunchy and couldn't possibly be eaten with a fork! But the customer loved it and **CRISPS** became all the rage!

In 1930, Ruth Graves Wakefield had to think fast. Her restaurant guests were finishing dinner and expected freshly baked cookies for dessert. But she didn't have the right baking chocolate. There was no time, so Ruth used the only type she had, chopped up into pieces. Instead of melting in the oven, the chocolate made **CHOCOLATE CHIPS**! A mistake that is now a cookie classic!

Frank Epperson was 11 when he realised one winter morning that he had accidentally left his soda-making kit outside overnight. The sugary liquid had frozen and the stick he had used for stirring was stuck. Thank goodness he forgot or we wouldn't have **ICE LOLLIES**!

Next time you're enjoying a cheese toastie, remember this: cheese may have been discovered by chance. Some have said that, thousands of years ago, a merchant from the Middle East carried milk inside a pouch made from a sheep's stomach . . . yum? Add the hot sun and the stomach's natural bacteria and bada boom – **THE EARLIEST FORM OF CHEESE!**

Even one of the greatest military commanders in history made mistakes now and again. General Hannibal was famous for military strategy that no one expected – but this sometimes came at a price. In 218 BC, he led his entire army across the Alps to surprise Rome with an attack from the North. It was so dangerously snowy and steep that thousands of men, horses and even a bunch of elephants **FELL OFF THE CLIFFS** in the process. Watch out!

It's easy to mess up under pressure – especially when a whole city is depending on you! In 1977, New York City's power supply was in danger of a black out, and it was up to one operator to fix it. He had to flip a series of switches, but he missed just one and BOOM! The city that never sleeps went dark for 25 long hours.

Ouch! My foot!
Is that you?
Where are we?
So dark!

In 2011, a 75-year-old woman BROKE THE INTERNET with a spade. She was digging for copper when she hit a massive underground cable that provided internet to most of Armenia and some parts of Georgia and Azerbaijan – cutting over three million people off for five hours.

Everyone FORGETS THEIR KEYS now and again – but this doesn't usually sink a ship as big as RMS Titanic. It's said that there was only one pair of binoculars on board, which could have helped the crew spot the dangerous iceberg sooner. But these were locked away, and the only person who had the key was working on another ship and had forgotten to leave it behind.

Some mistakes are made ON PURPOSE!

TO PROTECT YOUR WORK...

Some cartographers, or map-makers, use clever tricks to protect their work from being copied. They sneak the names of places that don't exist into their maps, on purpose, as a kind of signature. There are up to 100 **TRAP STREETS** in the London A-Z Map alone!

TO KEEP SECRETS...

Spies have always used secret codes to communicate – to protect top-secret information and to protect themselves from getting caught. There are endless ways to write a code. Say – this message on the left has a lot of spelling mistakes, doesn't it? What would happen if you wrote down each letter that's not supposed to be there?

OR FOR SUPERSTITION...
15
14
12
11
10
9
Have you ever noticed how some buildings don't have a 13th floor? You're not crazy – TRISKAIDEKAPHOBIA is the fear of the number 13 and some hotel rooms, building floors and locker doors skip it altogether just to be safe. In China, it's the 4th floor that's sometimes missing. Four is an unlucky number there, since the word for 4 sounds very similar to 'death'. Yikes!

ERRORS IN ART

In 2018, during a London art sale, a piece of artwork by Banksy was bought for one million pounds. Just seconds after, the work began to shred itself! Guards rushed to see what had gone wrong, but soon realised it had been done on purpose by the artist to make fun of the fancy art-buying process. Funnily enough, the unusual piece became even more valuable afterwards!

MISHAPS IN MUSIC
Musicians strive to get a strong reaction from their audience,
but in 1913, Russian composer Igor Stravinsky may have got more
than he bargained for. His ballet The Rite of Spring was so
MODERN AND SHOCKING that a riot broke out at the
Paris premiere! It took years for audiences to
understand what a remarkable work it is!

Collectors worldwide will drop serious dough for **RARE MISTAKES** that sometimes happen when things get made. From coins with two heads to toys with strange or missing parts – the weirder and rarer the better! There's a US stamp that went from being worth two dollars to nearly two million dollars, all because it was printed upside down.

It was challenging for this lady from England to forgive her husband for **THROWING AWAY HER 113 MILLION POUND WINNING LOTTERY TICKET**. It's no surprise she turned her house upside down looking for it. Although it never turned up, she did find a completely different winning ticket that her husband had also thrown in the bin – only for 10 pounds though.

But you could lose millions online too . . . if you don't keep your passwords safe. In 2021, an American programmer was close to losing 220 million dollars when he lost the password to a special digital bank account.

He only had two guesses left until he was locked out of his account forever . . .

THIS was supposed to be THAT!
Can you match these inventions with what they were supposed to be originally?

A When Alfred Fielding and Marc Chavannes sewed two shower curtains together, they thought they had made a fun new kind of **WALLPAPER** . . . I guess you could still use it that way. Might be a little noisy though.

B Richard James was a bit clumsy in his workshop, even when trying to figure out ways to keep things steady on **ROCKING SHIPS**. It's not every day that dropping springs on the ground leads to the invention of a bestselling kid's toy!

C Who knew a putty-like **WALLPAPER CLEANER** would become so fun to kids around the world?! The inventor couple Cleo and Noah McVicker certainly didn't!

D Edward Hass III was just trying to make a **MINT** that would help smokers smoke a little less. He never expected the collectible, delectable treat that it became instead!

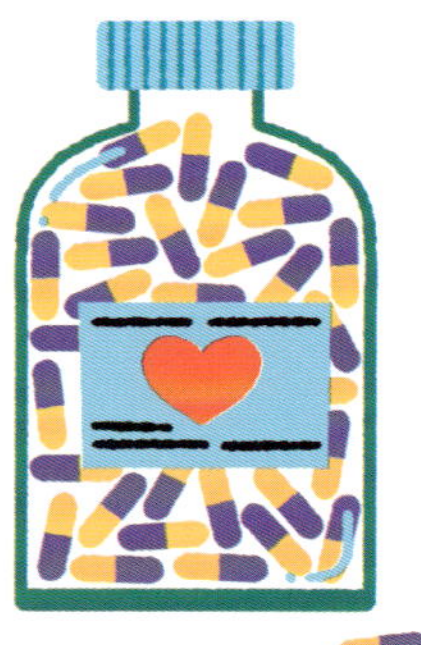

E A group of chemists panicked at first, but the unusual side effect to the **HEART MEDICINE** they were developing went from being a hairy situation to an incredible discovery!

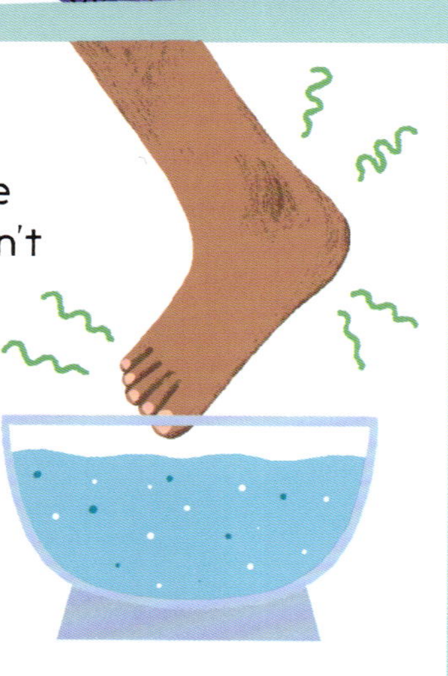

F Joseph Lister was beside himself. He simply couldn't believe that the stuff he had made to scrub floors and **CLEAN STINKY FEET** was now used to make your mouth smell fresh. Preposterous!

G Thomas Adams thought the tree sap he got from Mexico would be a great new kind of **RUBBER**, so he tried to make everything with the stuff. Toys, boots, you name it – all failures! Who knew failure could taste so good!

1
2
3
4
5
6
7

Solutions:
A-7
B-6
C-2
D-5
E-1
F-3
G-4

You never know what you might find when you're NOT looking . . .

Ever had something fall down the toilet by mistake? Now imagine, centuries later, future archeologists finding what you'd lost! That's what happened in 2012, when scientists excavated an **ANCIENT COMMUNITY TOILET** in France. Among the ancient poo, they found the **GOLDEN HAIRPIN** of Catherine de Medici, Queen of France in the 1500s!

COFFEE may have been discovered by dancing goats! As legend has it, an Ethiopian goat herder named Kaldi noticed his goats acting a little . . . strange. They were dancing and prancing about, full of energy, so he decided to investigate. When Kaldi tried the berries his goats had been eating, he too felt a pep in his step!

In 2015, a farmer in Michigan, USA, was working in his soybean fields when he was surprised to find a very large bone. When paleontologists did some digging, they discovered the **SKULL OF A WOOLLY MAMMOTH** – tusks and all! This was a super-important discovery that changed experts' records of how early these animals were around in North America. Also makes for a pretty awesome living room ornament.

Imagine digging down to find a face staring back at you – or **THOUSANDS OF FACES**! That's how farmers stumbled upon the life-size pottery soldiers of China's famous Terracotta Army. The 'City of the Dead' was built for China's first emperor when he was only 13 years old and it's almost as big as the city of Paris!

Yes, another toilet story! In 2001, one Italian man didn't know what he was getting into when he tried to fix his toilet. All he wanted was to find the broken pipe. Instead, his digging unearthed an OLD UNDERGROUND CITY beneath his house, dating back hundreds of years. Oh, and they also found the pipe.

Search engines make about 400 million pounds a year from mistakes we make when typing out website names online. Because this happens so often, the internet is full of **TYPOSQUATTING** websites, with names that are spelled *almost* exactly like famous ones. These sites are often full of Google's adverts, so even if you got there by accident, Google makes money!

. . . to outer space!

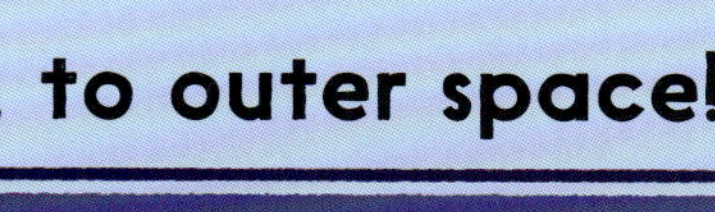

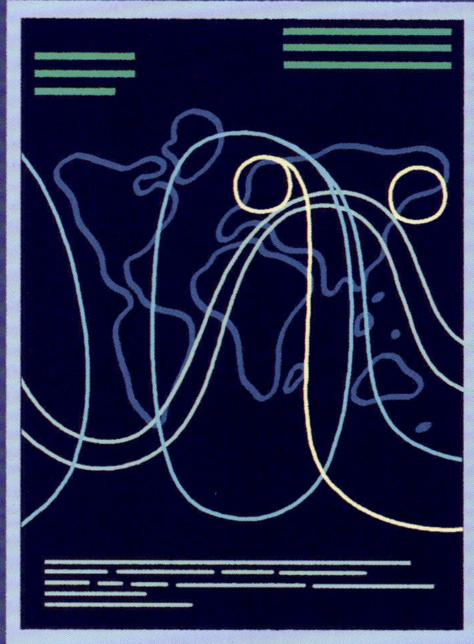

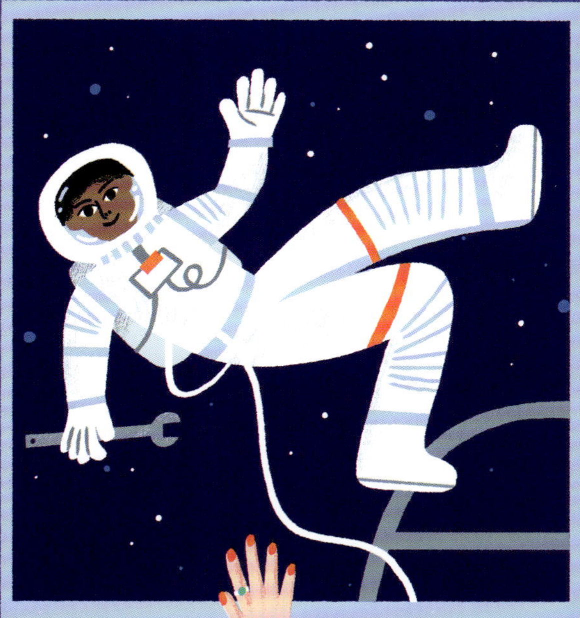

There's no escape from messing up – even out here! In 1999, a team of NASA engineers built the Mars Orbiter and after almost 10 months of travel, the **SPACECRAFT** made it to Mars. But then it vanished. No one knows where it went. But they do know that some engineers had been using **INCHES** to navigate, while others used **METRES** or **MILLIMETRES**. No one is too smart to make mistakes – even rocket scientists!

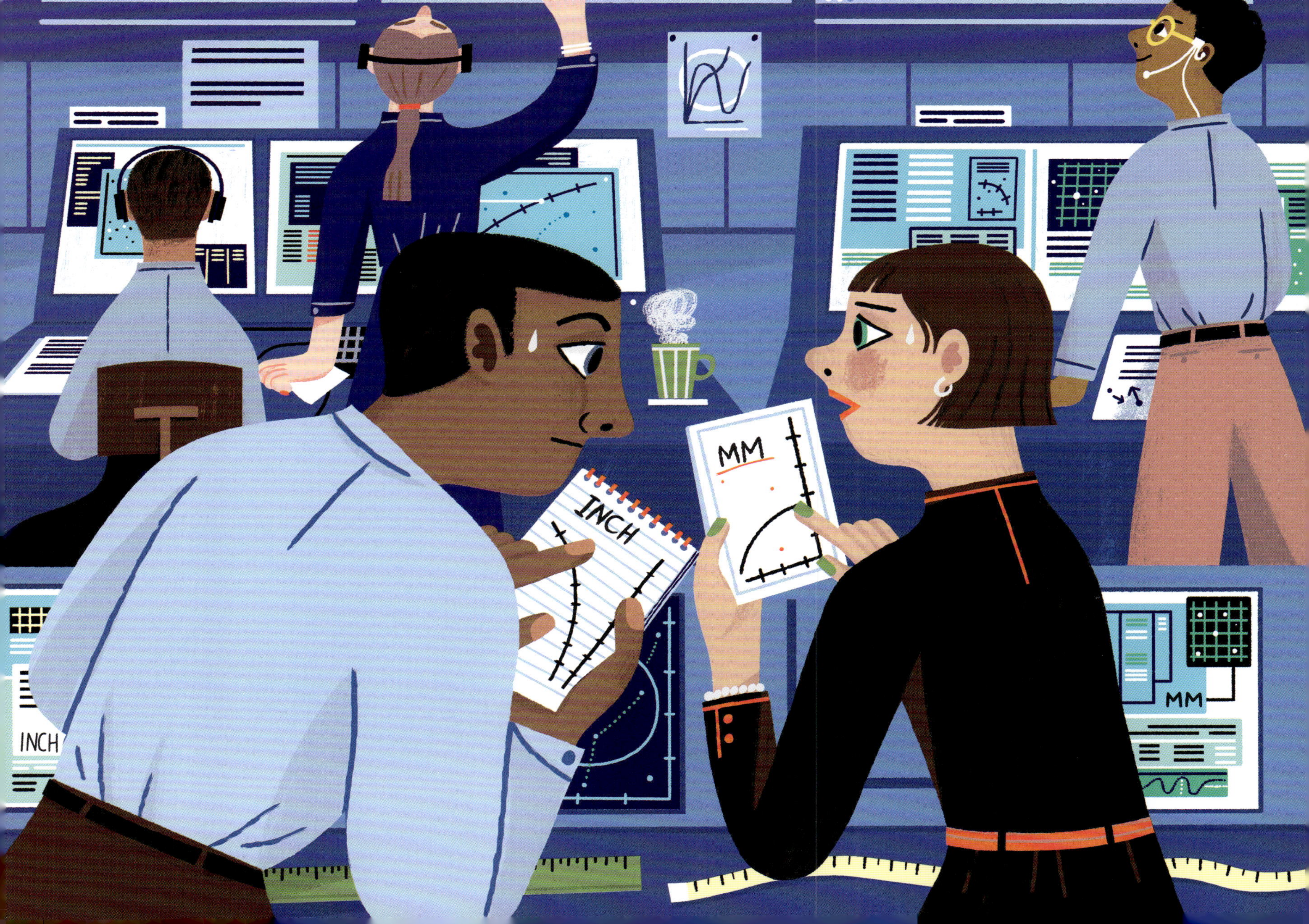

Sometimes a BOLD IDEA can lead to trouble . . .

Around the year 1010, a monk named Eilmer was inspired to strap a **MASSIVE PAIR OF WINGS** to his body and throw himself off the tippy top of Malmesbury Abbey in the UK. And so he did – and broke both his legs. But it was totally worth it! This was the first ever recorded attempt at human flight! Right, Eilmer?

Centuries later, a Californian man known as Lawn Chair Larry decided to fly nearly 5,000 metres into the air in a lawn chair attached to **OVER 40 HELIUM-FILLED WEATHER BALLOONS.** Believe it or not, a whole bunch of mistakes were made along the way – including forgetting to warn air traffic control and almost getting hit by a plane.

The scientist and politician Benjamin Franklin conducted all sorts of experiments with electricity, including trying to cook a Thanksgiving turkey by electrocuting it. It worked! It was apparently deliciously tender, but so was Ben Franklin, who zapped himself in the process. Mmm . . . **FRANKLINFURTERS**?

Nothing says celebration quite like **FIREWORKS**, but the man who first set them off probably didn't feel very festive. Over 2,000 years ago, a Chinese alchemist was experimenting with a combination of charcoal and minerals such as sulphur and saltpetre, in the hopes of creating a substance to make him live forever. Ironically, he had created the opposite – and with a BANG, gunpowder was born.

Have you ever mistaken something for fact?
Sometimes things you THINK you know are actually wrong!

It can be a beautiful thing to find out you were wrong. Correcting old information with new discoveries brings us closer to the truth!

Recent studies have shown that dinosaurs weren't all scaly – some had feathers like GIANT CHICKENS!

Ostriches DON'T ACTUALLY BURY THEIR HEADS in the sand when they're scared. But they do dig holes to bury their eggs, and stick their heads in to check on the little ones from time to time.

The white marble ancient Greek sculptures you see in museums were actually SUPER COLOURFUL back in their day. Most of their paint has just worn off over the years.

Lots of people believe that bats are blind. In fact, not only do they use a special sound-based sense called ECHOLOCATION to help them hunt in the dark, but they also can see rather well.

BATS

Think you only have 5 SENSES? Think again! Some scientists think there are actually OVER 20, including balance, hunger, pain and even knowing how to find the tip of your nose in the dark!

so powerful...

SWALLOWING CHEWING GUM is gross and not a good idea. BUT it's a myth that it will stay in your body for seven years. The gum takes the same amount of time to pass through your digestive system as other things you snack on.

STRAWBERRIES aren't actually berries, but bananas and avocados are.

THE TOWER OF PISA in Italy was never meant to lean. When construction started in 1173, nobody realised the soft ground wouldn't be able to support its weight. By the time builders reached the top, hundreds of years later, the lean was so intense that architects from all over the world tried to fix it. It was finally made stable in 2008.

There's a beautiful constellation mural across the ceiling of New York City's **GRAND CENTRAL TRAIN STATION.** The only problem is it was painted completely backwards. During construction in 1913, the plans were held up incorrectly, with west facing east and east facing west. Oops!

You're taking a gamble on going to **LAS VEGAS**! At least the guests of the Vdara Hotel and Spa felt that way. Opening in 2009, the hotel stood out with its unique curved shape. Fun! Except that this created a giant magnifying-glass effect that shot a laser-beam-like concentration of sunlight straight towards the hotel pool! The area got so hot that plastic bags and cups melted, and some guests were seriously sunburned! It's no wonder locals call it "The Death Ray".

What a day it was when the **MILLENNIUM BRIDGE** in London finally opened up to the public in 2000! What could be more exciting? How about the tiny rhythmic footsteps of pedestrians accidentally causing the entire bridge to sway back and forth, like a theme-park ride . . . Oops!

MESSING UP is such a normal part of everyday life that we even have tools to help!

Who better to show us around than Joseph Priestley, the chemist who literally invented the rubber?

Joseph made some of his most important discoveries **BY ACCIDENT**! Once he knocked over some mercury and found a gas called sulphur dioxide, used today to make dried fruit. He also discovered oxygen **AND DIDN'T EVEN KNOW IT**. If he hadn't got some experiments wrong, his research couldn't have been used by others to later get it right!

In the 1950s, Bette Nesmith Graham was a secretary in Texas, USA. At the time, it was very difficult to correct mistakes made on a typewriter, until one day – it clicked! Why couldn't you just paint over them? Bette secretly started using a tiny bottle of white paint and her **LIQUID PAPER** soon caught on.

Some **COMPUTER PROGRAMS** will help to fix spelling mistakes when you're typing. However, they can sometimes replace a typo with the wrong word, making a new mistake altogether!

Long before electronic teleprompters, there were people called **PROMPTERS** whose jobs depended on people making mistakes! From a little window at the front of the stage, the prompter would follow the script during a performance and whisper lines to actors if they got stuck. Now if only we could get these prompters in classrooms . . .

MNEMONICS are a useful tool and a fun way to help you remember things – hopefully without getting them wrong. The idea is to remember just one saying which will remind you about the other words. Pretty clever, huh!

Some mnemonics help you avoid spelling mistakes. It really helps our spelling to remember to "never believe a lie", that "we hear with our ear" or that "there's a rat in separate". Do you know who Roy G. Biv is? He's the guy who helps you remember the colours of the rainbow! Red, orange, yellow, green, blue, indigo, violet. Thanks, Roy!

When life gives you lemons,
make . . . pink lemonade?
Here's how to make
THE BEST OUT OF SOMETHING
going wrong!

There are lots of stories about where **PINK LEMONADE** came from – and many start at the circus! One story says that someone accidentally knocked a box of red cinnamon sweets into regular lemonade. Another says that someone found a bucket of dirty water that a performer had used to wash their pink tights in and sold it as **STRAWBERRY LEMONADE**. Yum?

In 1904, Ernest Hamwi was selling delicious Syrian desserts when he noticed a nearby ice-cream seller had run out of bowls. This gave Ernest an idea. He folded one of the waffle-like pastries he was selling into a cone and handed it over. **ICE CREAM AND ITS CONE** have been inseparable ever since!

Walter Hunt was a brilliant inventor, but one of his best creations happened by accident. One day in 1949, he was fiddling with a piece of metal wire while thinking about something else, twisting and turning it, until he realised that it had become something quite useful . . . the world's first **SAFETY PIN**!

After a hike in the Alps, Swiss engineer George de Mestral noticed that his clothes and his dog were covered in small sticky seeds called burrs. He soon realised they were actually clinging on with tiny hooks. This gave him the idea to create a **HOOK AND LOOP FASTENING SYSTEM** which is used everywhere today – from shoes to spacesuits!

Spencer Silver failed in 1968. He was supposed to be developing a super-strong glue, but instead he made a glue that was just as easy to unstick again. It wasn't until 10 years later that a colleague had the idea of using it for something else – and hey presto, we got the **STICKY-NOTE**!

Look at this BEAUTIFUL MESS! Sometimes being untidy can lead to incredible inventions . . .
Can you match the mess to the discovery?

A OK, perhaps my workspace is a tad messy . . . but I'm a very busy man! I don't have the time to wash my hands before every single treat! And you're welcome, by the way – you wouldn't have **artificial sweetener** if I had!

B If my assistant hadn't accidentally spilled rubber chemicals on our co-worker's shoes, I would never have developed one of the most successful liquid-repelling products to protect fabrics and carpets from **stains**.

3

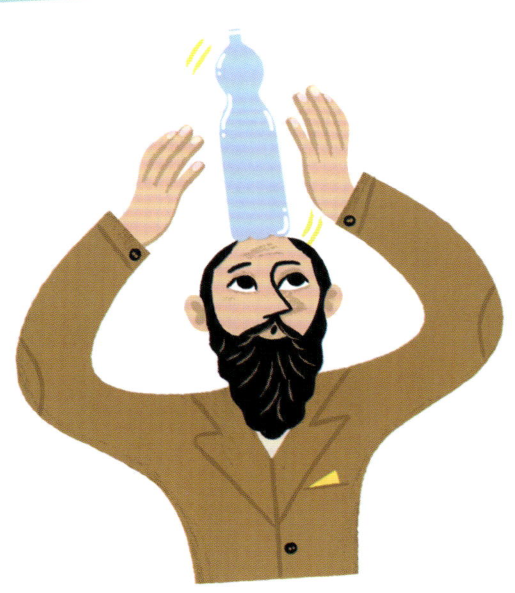

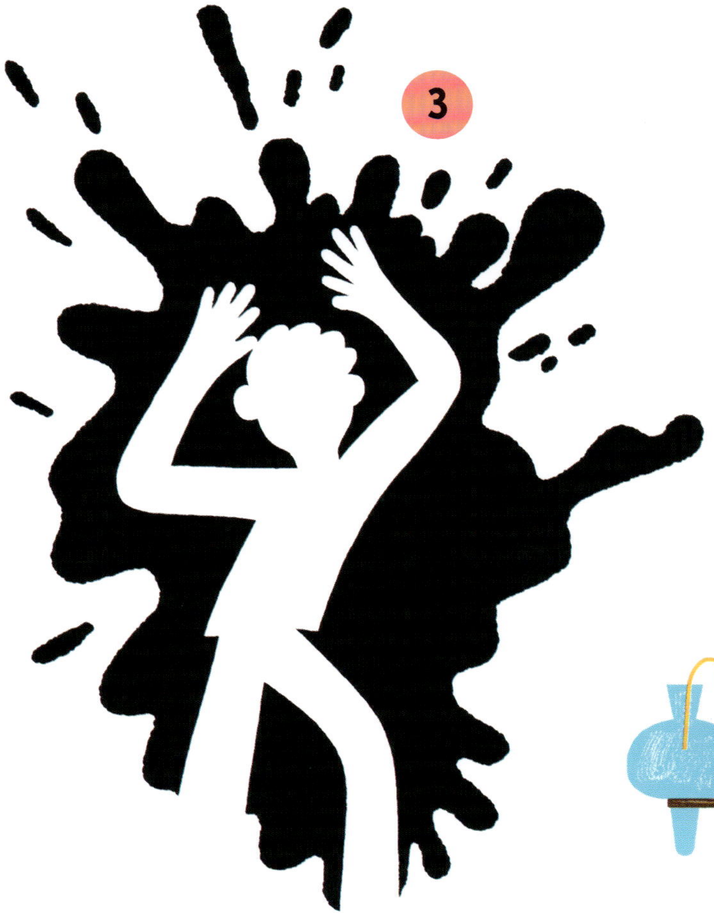

4

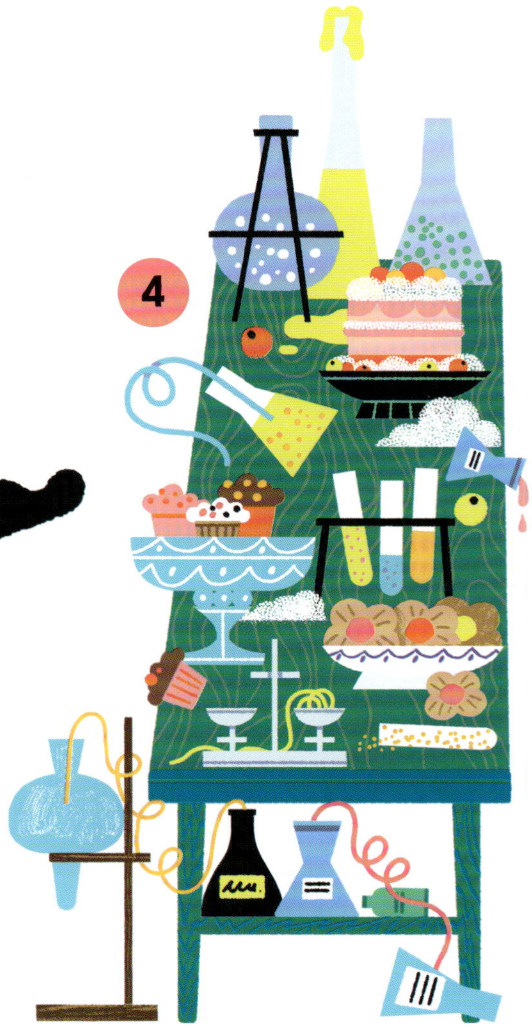

5

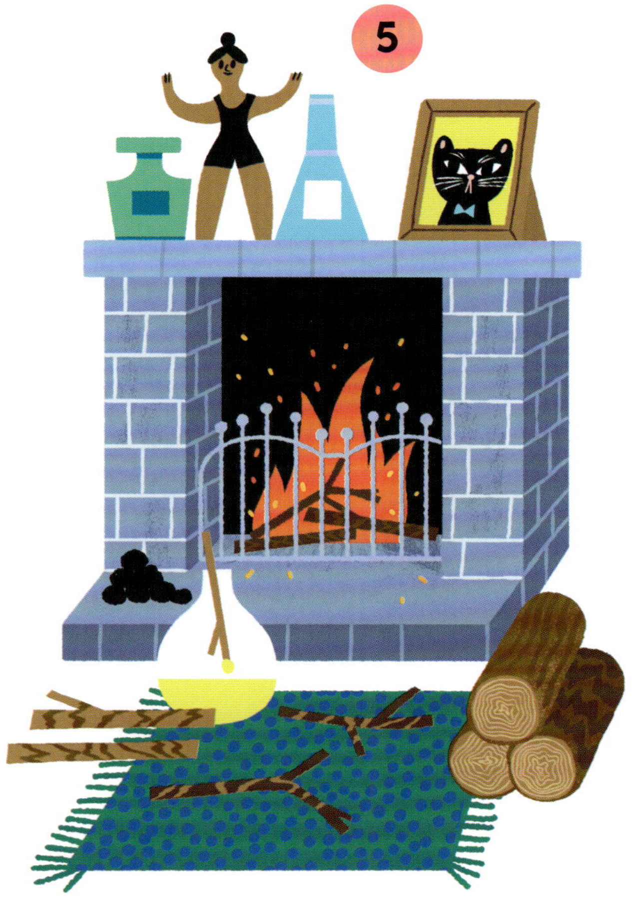

C If I hadn't spilled pools of dangerous chemicals around my workstation willy-nilly, I would never have accidentally invented **plastic**!

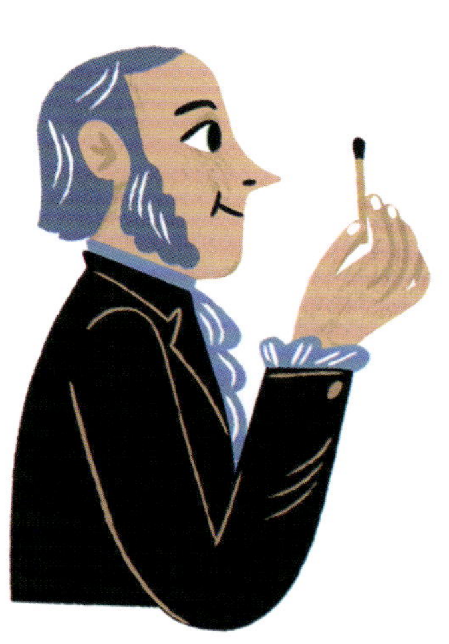

D It's a good thing I scraped the blob of equally dangerous chemicals off my mixing stick, or you'd all be stuck trying to light a fire without **matches**!

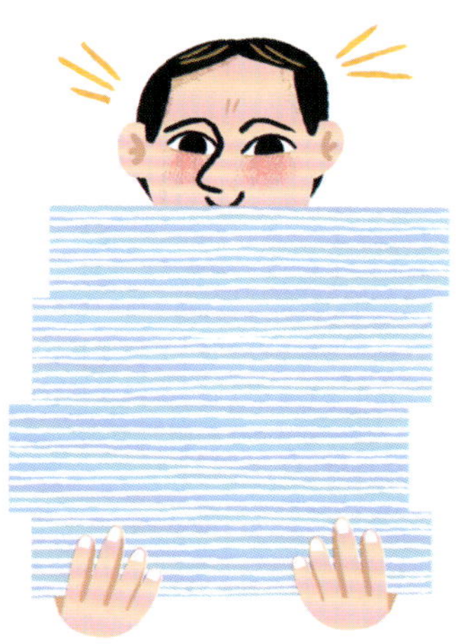

E Would you be able to **print** out those important documents if I hadn't accidentally left my iron on a pen, causing ink to explode everywhere? I think not!

Solutions: 1-C, 2-B, 3-E, 4-A, 5-D

Just remember . . . NEXT TIME
you make a mistake, DON'T WORRY.
Give yourself a high five instead.
It's a sign you're learning something new.
HOW EXCITING!

Sometimes, mistakes are a chance to have new ideas
that you would never have thought of on purpose!
Mistakes can sometimes be a little bit scary, but we all
make them – even grown-ups. It's what humans do.
How else would you grow up to become, well – YOU!
No one else messes up the way you do!

What incredible mistake
MISTAKE
did you make today?

GLUE